Open Heart Surgery

Poems and Other Revelations

By Carlos Robinson

ODF Publishing House

Table of Contents

Open Heart Surgery

The first time they performed the operation on me was more of an experiment. I was 11 years old. Just a boy with little or no understanding of what they were trying to achieve. Being so young I really didn't care what their purpose was. Of course they knew. I was too ambitious and head strong. Too mobile and energetic to worry about the repercussions of the heart surgery they had only just begun to perform on me at that time but it now seems to have been going on forever.

At the time the poking and prodding of my flesh and internal makeup only caused humorous, untainted effort's to sustain the unknowing innocence I held onto versus their very mature, immaculate culture of unpolished surgeons. I rejected their every attempt to conform me physically, emotionally or however they deemed for me to respond. And with each rejection came many painful days that washed away in childish behavior; in acts of defiance.

It would be years before they operated again. I rushed into adolescence with a fervor that shielded me from their taunts and pleas to just lay still. Now I withstood stronger doses of anesthetics to the point I'd become oblivious to pain. So I sought to weaken their hearts by not letting them into mine. But I found out no man is immune to their probing of his being. In due time we give in; make ourselves susceptible to their different forms of operating. See, as a teen the operations became studies with a broad range of topics like pride, humiliation, jealousy, but most importantly, love. However the main course of study to me was always pain. Every operation hurt more than the last until I finally in desperation cried out for the pain to stop!

That was the last time they operated on me and I lay there asking "why?" But now as an older gentleman, I believe "why" isn't for any man to know. Just take heed that they were preparing me for a fate that only out of exuberance to love would often break my heart again and again and again. So now each surgery done details my seemingly lonely existence and for a time repairs my heart enough that I feel the joy of love. Most times the emptiness fades until a new surgeon comes along and I willingly agree to let them operate on me. Only now as a women can, not the little girls that they once were. Every man needs to undergo open heart surgery to understand the meaning of the poems in his head and all the other revelations on love.

Poetic Infusion

"What is this I write and sometimes
speak?"   Poetry?

"What is poetry?"   A poem?

"What then is a poem but spoken or written
word's?"   Ahhhh.....

"Word's are meaningless unless they're understood and these I
speak are meant to be clearly recognized as they should.

To give them life as they form from the very breaths I take.
They are bodies of vowel's and syllables. Limbs of pronunciations
for every move I make.

These words are my thought process, my innermost emotions.
The feelings I have to describe. They are my anger, my happiness;
those things that are apparent to me but from you I can easily hide.

So I write and recite fervently to get my words across. Not just
because my life is words but because these words are my life and
without meaning I am lost.

I don't do this because I can. I do it because I have to.

I have to understand. I have to live! I have to write to express!
To be FREE!!

As I want others to grasp, be enthused by, amazed at...... my life!
In its simplicity, its diversity. Spoken through...... poetry."

Waiting on Zero

"Even though I knew she wouldn't come back I waited with anticipation anyway; such a bored fool. But I say, "I'm cool! If she don't return then it's her loss!" when I know I will never hear from Zero again. For some reason this eases the fact I've always known she didn't love me as I hoped she did."

Untitled: I

"What manner of fool doth lay down arms when faced with loves relentless attack?

Oh far winds that gale against flesh, blow thee away from the battlefield to a more peaceful place where hearts can be free. But why is there such disdain for the tainted mercies of inhumane warfare, when lust, unconquered, rampages over yearning emotions. Needing so desperately to be felt and maintained.

Under starry sky looking to the far heavens for answers to loves impending questions. Knowing her fury will certainly claim many victims within her wrath.

And yet..... Yet dear God of grace, dare we seek loves everlasting embrace even though unbeatable odds prevail? Then suddenly as sun courageously sets to rest itself under night's blanket of dark moonless sky; so does the weary warrior. Again left alone, stifled by loneliness and pain, waiting anxiously with eyes closed for no restful sleep can penetrate ones broken heart. Yes anxiously looking to the east for the rising brightness of a new day and the battle shall without fail rage once more.

I cringe from mistakes made mountainously enough that I should know not to make them again. Still I do with hope that next time I take the stance to fight.

That just maybe the lessons learned will spare me from loves fiery harm."

My Face....

I looked upon the aura of love and it called my name as if it has known me all my life. "Beautiful." that's what love called me with a voice so soft and demure. And like a surging wave against a fading shore I melted with tears.

"Why do you cry oh GREAT man of emotion? Have I offended thee in someway by stating your wondrous power to be as God created you to be?" Loves question struck discord within my soul because I never saw myself as beautiful and would not allow anyone else to see it either because then they would see it as weakness.

"Or do you cry from the pain of living your life and not until now knowing just who you really are as a man?" love continued.

In anger I shouted out from the very top of tainted lungs," I NEVER CRIED FOR LOVE BUT SURELY FROM THE PAIN! I NEVER CRIED FROM JOY, BUT SURELY FROM DISDAIN! WHAT IS IT YOU WANT FROM ME!?!"

And without a seconds hesitation loves answer is this...." I have never wanted anything of you that you're not capable to give."....so strong her voice yet serene.

I began to sob woefully. Lamenting the distress of many years spent in loneliness. I bowed my head in shame and love tenderly lifted it then very gently like falling flakes of snow kissed my lips with a passion that calmed me for the moment; my heart pounding hard like drummers of some ancient ritual signifying the approaching battle to all surrounding tribes. I now smiled so brightly with confidence and pride! My longing for love had been given reprieve..... My emotions had finally been set..... Free, if only for that moment in time.

Years have passed since that encounter and when I thought that day was merely a dream I realize now it wasn't. Love still kisses me and calls my name "Beautiful". It comforts me even though loneliness has built a prison around my heart.

Love is always there. Waiting for me to accept it's real and to invite her into my life. Without being afraid or feeling unworthy to receive such a blessing. Love is everywhere and in everything but it can not be seen purely with carnal eyes. No..... this kind of love can only be seen with the eyes of one's heart."

Peppermint Patty

Sometimes people will come and go from our lives but what we shared will always remain. Sometimes we reach out for what we may think is love but life won't let us know if what we think is real or just a foolish dream.

But the truth is that in the end we have been given that chance to find a friend. So now you're gone and what have we accomplished? What kind of man would I be if I just let you go, after sharing my heart with you?

Today there's a wrinkle of pain that has returned to my face. I don't know why this hurts so much. I don't know why I take the blame. I don't know why I hope you'll see that you mean the world to me or that if I let you go I'll be the one left all alone.

I know that what I deem a woman to be in my life may seem impossible. Experiences have shown me that the kind of unconditional love I desire is so hard to attain. There's just too much any woman will have to fore go.

I know that the woman I need and saw in you are the same but maybe the man you need I can never be? Maybe I was a fool for believing you could be my "woman" but in the annals of my mind it was worth being a fool to find out."

May I be excused......

I could never say "I'm sorry." I could never accept being hurt in my heart. I talk too much sometimes to get my point across, when maybe it's not worth the time.

I've opened up my life like a jagged can filled with worms. I've told things about me to people that never knew me, nor do they truly care. I've experienced the pain and torment of loss and held it in because my pride wouldn't let me share.

I have said "I LOVE YOU" so many fucking times that I wonder is there that much love to give?! I've cried so many tears. I hope that no one ask me to be a friend because that space is long occupied by fear.

I really don't deserve to be hurt anymore but if I put myself in harms way then whose fault is it? I really don't deserve to be alive but miraculously God doesn't see things as I do so here I live and hurt and smile and feel.

"AND WHAT'S THE POINT SISSY BOY!?"

"CAN'T I JUST VENT!? CAN'T I JUST ONE TIME.... stop!" Be patient and wait for the miracle to manifest? Worry not that it won't materialize. Have faith that good things will come if I only wait?

Growing up then old is a hard thing to do but it is inevitable long as we live. But sooner or later I'll die and this will all be someone else's life someone else's memory........"

Goodbye?

Parting words are such sweet sorrow.

Most will burn the heart come sunrise tomorrow.

Bringing to remembrance all that's been said.

One will either smile or cry, be happy or sad, because of the memories that remain in one's head.

To hear "goodbye" no matter what tone of voice is used,

sounds so final in all it's intent and most times leaves the heart well bruised.

But to say "goodnight" gives hope that one can see many "good" nights to come,

There is no anger, no malice to go undone.

Dare we part from a lover's life forever?

Then it will serve to be haunted with goodbye's finality that touches the soul

because the last we say will be the first we shall always remember.

Sweetly "goodnight" kisses the cheek and keeps us hanging on.

Even though sorrow accompanies our hearts until the next time we talk, and on that day behold ! Then brand new "good nights" are born.

When God Created Woman

I said, "This isn't worth it anymore. Love. Man that shit will drive a man to murder or suicide! Oh, no not me! Never again!". I can't even point a finger at myself. Just a thought, because damn. I meet a woman and swear "she's the one"! Oh man this is it LOS!!! She's beautiful, smart, witty, self assured, great in bed, understanding, a real ass friend, responsible, kind, and love's me uncon------oops! Where'd she go!? Many may not understand me. Many may think I'm foolish bordering on crazy! Uh huh, yeah I see it in the way you look at me when I come strutting around with my head in the clouds (or is it up my ass?!) because there is a new woman in my life. You think I don't hear the comments like, "poor asshole thinks he's in love again", or "poor asshole thinks she really love's him". Damn! Can you just lift a brother up once instead of tearing down his hopes and dreams?! That may very well be the answer. Maybe I put too much into discovering if the dream can come true rather than just admit that nothing comes to dreamers but dreams.

Hmmmmm... Don't give up. Don't lose faith. Don't stop believing in love or women's ability to love unconditionally. Shit, what is unconditional anyways? Everything has to have conditions. Why not love? Why not love......?

When love isn't enough

I try so hard to be sensitive to love. Opening up that place in my heart where even I am really afraid to venture because of all the disappointments faced and lived through. Love has not been a good friend to me. I've lost more than I've gained; still I have hope for that one glimmer of what a real lasting, meaningful and blessed relationship will be like in my life. If only I could say I never had the chance to love then maybe I could understand why love keeps eluding me. I've had many opportunities for love. I also realize that it is more than just saying, "I love you", or being in someone's life only as a physical presence.

Maybe if I didn't know love then I wouldn't expect it to return to my heart because I could not understand what this powerful emotion entails and requires of me as a man. Just maybe if I didn't know love then I wouldn't feel the hurt and loneliness of it's disappearing acts. Just maybe my first love would be here with me now assuring me that everything will be alright.

Angels

Okay so we have reached this fork in the road where love is as needed as life and life is predicated by the love we share with angels. I mean, isn't it a rare opportunity to live in an earthly vessel yet, still entertain the spiritual influences along the way? Angels. Ones we meet and never see again; ones that become part of our lives forever. You will know if you've ever been touched..........by an angel.

Untitled II

I'm not in love.

I can't be in love, not with a memory.

There is no soft walnut brown skin to hold.

No shape, no smell, no taste. No heart to tenderly mold.

I'm not in love with a memory; it's just not the same.

How can I expect a memory to love me, make love to me?

When I am hooked to a ball and chain and memory has no key.

Still I think about you every night baby.

Wanting you here with me so bad I feel I'm going crazy.

I don't want to think that I meant nothing to you but then I have to wonder if I meant anything at all.

I don't want to keep hoping that you will return and if you are hoping the same thing too.

I don't want to think about you but there is nothing else I'd rather do.

I'm not in love. This isn't real. Not a memory, not even close to what and how I feel.

I miss you......I miss you...........I...............miss.................you.

There for me

I can't help wondering sometimes who's going to be here for me when I really need someone to be? I know there are people in my life that come around on their time. I'm not talking about them because a time will come when I won't be able to have hope that they will show. Neither will I be able to search them out. So I can't help wondering on days like this, such as days past, who's going to be here for me when I really need someone to be?

I keep lying to myself that I don't need anyone, or that I'm just fine by myself. But truth is I know I'm lying because loneliness constantly reminds me of the truth that as I go on there will be days when I need someone to comfort me; someone to give me emotional and physical support. And even though I get so much from God spiritually, I'm still human and need the kind of things humans give each other as well. Love being the most important.

Its funny how I have so many to love but no one I can claim as a love of my own. Thus I know there is no one in my life right now that I can hold confidence in being there for me when I really need someone to be.

So today I hurt inside. Emptiness won't leave me alone. I realize I'm so far from what I can for sure call home. I'm so far from being in a lover's heart. I can't fool myself and the pain of truth is getting harder each day to fake. So I write to give my soul peace. Just to talk and for a page or two ease my mind. It's what I've done for years now. Even though it sometimes isn't enough especially being I have no answers. My heart has no relief and right now more so than ever before I can't help wondering, who's going to be here for me when I really need someone to be?

My Heart is Heavy

When I know your heart is troubled, I too am engulfed by your pain. Because you are the woman I love. Without your happiness to inspire my life, my own happiness can be distant; even mundane.

I feel the soulful tears you cry. Like thousand pound weights they fall upon my heart. Hard tears of heaviness that I sometimes dread will tear us apart. But as your man I'm here baby.

I give you my heart filled by the joy you bring to my soul in exchange for your sadness and fears; because I love you. I share my world with you because it is in my world that the beauty of your smile is queen. So in your time of despair, to see you smile from the hope of real love, having a cleansed soul and freedom, I take the throne in your heart shining through as your king.

I will fight the long war, do whatever it takes to help you see the joy you so deserve. I am here to hold your hand and guide you as we both feel loves courage. Without failure or ceasing I'll give you my love and that is how I intend to prove these words.

Heat

Soft kisses with luscious full lips.

Gentle touches caressing the skin.

Gazing into eyes that peer beyond the flesh, much deeper into ones soul.

Two embracing bodies moving systematically with the fluidity of a greatly inspired sonata.

Passions erupting like a volcanoes fury with each thrust.

Moans of pleasure resonating from within a chasm of mortal ecstasy.

Sounds so enticing, igniting lust' so fiery that to engage in sexual stimulation can not be overlooked.

Two hearts beating rhythmically as one.

Gasp of breath warm and soothing.

Her moisture turning physically to drenching wetness.

Sounds of bodies pumping, gyrating, penetrating, slapping against each other.

Hardness against softness.

Deep and pounding.

Slowly then faster.

Tensing to the point only spasmodic tics between two muscular beings remain, signifying the height of orgasmic bliss.

With one....... harsh........ relieving heave......

To collapse, melting together.

Throbbing, pulsating. They tighten.

Small pushes releasing every drop of energy, of lust, of passion.

As the embrace of satisfaction encompasses two beings and for that one moment there is love, either from how good it felt or because the heart wants to feel.

Computer Love

Another lonely night and I sit here at the keyboard staring into the blankness of my monitors screen. Typing a conversation I would have with the ghost of a woman I long to be with....

To lay in her arms and make love to her until we both fall asleep. That, just perchance being physically spent, I will be allowed to sleep without the nightmare of my empty heart yearning for her love....

To feel her warmth and be comforted by her touches upon my skin, the way her spirit awakens my passion and soothes my soul; and, wanting to hear her say, "I love you Carlos...so very much." Finding the assurance of love in her words even though this ghost girl is merely a fantasy I relish in cyberspace.

Today

I don't put much faith in tomorrow. As God will have it, all I can do is hope it will come.

Thus my desire rest assured in today. Right now. With each second that passes and I am still alive, I give thanks to whom all life derives from.

I'm thankful today for each achievement. For each step I did not make in vain.

I'm thankful for the days of sunshine that warms my skin and helps all things to grow, even for the days of rain.

I see life today because it is today I am afforded to live.

I am thankful for the blessings I receive, even for those I give.

Today I cry.

Today I smile.

Today I have things that won't be here after awhile.

Today I have friends.

Today I am alone.

Today I am a king sitting proud upon my throne.

I have faith today, right now, God has seen me through.

Faith that today, right now, I've done as God so willed me to do.

And when I fall on my knees to pray, it will be for one more opportunity to live just one more today.

But if it doesn't come for me then I only hope to end up in a place like today where my soul can live and be free.

HMMMMMMMM.......

Monday 3/17/2007 1:31pm

I have known only one Caucasian woman that I would even consider being in my life as anything other than a sex toy...... until today. For me white women were never the type or race that I would marry or want to spend the rest of my life with. Not that I am prejudice or racially motivated, just that I always wanted to believe no woman outside my ethnicity would be deserving of this amount of affection from me. Love. Of course I have noticed them before from an emotional distance. Hell, I even dated two or three but not once did I consider seriously spending the rest of my days with one as my wife..... until today!

It was kind of funny how I sensed someone watching me. Not once but twice, maybe the entire time I shopped!? I really don't know about the "before" all I do know is when I realized she was paying me attention, at that very moment she acquired mine as well. I was instantly taken by her walk; the self assured swagger of her body; the brightness of her green eyes and beautifully sparkling smile. She wasn't like the other white woman I had seen. She had been blessed with the very anatomy God can bestow a woman of Caucasian stature. Everything about her stated her freedom to be the woman she is and this captivated me.

So after remembering who I am, a man, of course, I let instinct lead ms to approach and talk to her and now and the rest is history. BUT! Here's the kicker.... I can't remember how or when it happened that these women became more than sexual objects to me. All I know is white women to me are now the same as all other women of this world have always been..... They are individual people of color. I can desire them in my life to fulfill my heart and give me happiness as any other woman can, but only if I allow them to be the women they are. Not the women I saw them as before.

"If I could cry 4 love, I'd cry 4 losing U"

I was raised with the belief that a man isn't suppose 2 cry. Don't wear my emotions on my sleeve and definitely NEVER EVER fall n love!

So now when I'm n pain, I lock it deep n'side and it turns to anger. N'stead of crying out I keep it and it fester's like a cancerous lesion n my soul.

U said, "I will NEVER leave u, my lover" and I believed this. U said, "U'll learn 2 unlock the love u have n'side my lover finally easing the pain and anger." u said it would b good 4 me.U lied 2 me!!

Still, I held on2 ideas of the life a man is suppose 2 live and the way he is to live it! But I knew i could not hold on2 u while continuing 2 live that way.

Even as u walked out of my life and heart. Even as I fought n'wardly against running and falling on my knees b4 u imploring u not 2 go! I could not because the weight I carry of rejection is far heavier than my need 2 b seen as a man.

And so I say, "Love caused my pain!!" I'd blame it for the tears I felt but dared not shed from my eyes. I'd blame love 4 losing u. I'd blame u 4 loving me. I'd blame myself 4 even thinking I could love u n return..... without giving my heart the chance 2 learn how.

Hurt

Wow I really hurt sometimes. I'm only human and there will be days that just plain suck! Yet I am grateful to be alive even in pain. Whether mental, physical, emotional, or spiritual, at least I am alive. Many are out there that understand what it truly is to be grateful for life. I just happen to be one. I never thought wanting to live would be so demanding; so admired.

There are those that may read this and are about to cash in their chips (so to speak). Just give up. Well if there is one thing I can say that may help change your mind, it is this.... "I too have been through the fire of a life less ordinary; the trials and tribulations, the misguided mistakes; abuses too wrought in evil to describe. But through it all I am grateful because each experience prepared me for what I live with and through today. So don't give up. Our best days are still to come if we just hold on and have faith that once on the other side everything will be alright, even if only for a little while. Surely as we live and travel down this road called life, there is construction going on just up the way that will try and block, slowdown, or make us want to stop travelling. But we must keep moving on toward the mark of that higher calling where this will not matter anymore but what we did to survive will be what someone else needs to look at in order for them to do the same."

"Live on........"

My Song

We all want that one song that just describes our life. That melodic tune we can dance to and be free to act as we are without being judged or second guessed. My song; It owns my life. It touches my heart in places that no human can or dares to be; that deep inside my being. Where did it all go? The days of romance, hanging out with no intentions other than to laugh and play..... have fun? Why has this become so disenchanting? Like we are all just playing some kind of game that only one person knows the rules to or makes them up as they go.

My song is irregular in its beat like a good fusion jazz tune of bass, drums, piano, and horns. Pinging and clambering about in no particular cadence but still so very together. Making my feet tap with all the vibrancy of the sun at high noon. My heart beats out of sync yet keeps track with the rhythms of existence. When I hear it I can't help feel apart from the world because it is there I am king in a kingdom created specially for me; a kingdom where everyone is faithful, caring, sexual, devoted, responsible and kind. In my song I am more than what life has afforded me to be. I have no limits, no fears, no inhibitions...... I can be me.

My song gives me the chance to find love and treasure it. A love that only comes to those that have earned it's presence in our hearts. A love that does not see my illness because all it cares about is who I am as a person. In my song I can cry because I am tired of waiting for my ending to come and I am afraid it will come too soon. I can cry because though I present this strong, optimistic man on the outside, inside the fear of death awaiting me envelopes my soul. My song allows me to believe no one blames me for sometimes wanting to give up. I hear the melody and it sounds soooooo sweet!!! My song tells me it is alright telling someone, "I love you" because I have the courage to be sensitive and open. There is no rejection only postponement.

My song...... gives me more than I care to allow.

My song...... tells me "NO!" when all I want to hear is yes.

My song...... whispers, "it's going to be alright." and I believe it will.

This is my song. Listen to it if you will and if you really can hear the melody I'm sure you can understand me when I say that even though it is my song it is yours also, but in a different key.

We should have just said "Goodbye"

We held each other loosely but tight enough to feel this was the end. Our hearts pounding inside, words could not express how we felt knowing our love for this time has to end. I could see in your eyes you were cursing my existence. Like dew drops falling from moistened leaves you cursed me. How could I make love to you after this?

Because I don't know better I rush you into bed even though there was no more fire in our kisses.

We couldn't make love. The only thing left was to perform the ritual of sex. Grunting and grinding like two people angry at our lives; we try so desperately to meld but the separation of our hearts was more than we could bear.

Then your tears caressed my face as we reached an orgasm that was nothing short of hurt for all the years. Now we did not care.

We lay there wondering what next? You cried more intense. I held you to console your breaking spirit when it was mine that needed to just this last time feel that you still loved me. But there was nothing left. To say we can still be friends was an insult but the only words of consolation afforded trying to find a way out because now we must adjust to being free. So we stood by idling cars afraid that once we entered the journey would take us farther than we cared to be apart.

There was no way to escape the inevitable misery of breaking up. It's better this way. Now we can give love a well deserved and needed fresh start.

Suddenly as we were about to go our individual ways, I took the moment to steal these words from somewhere back in my mind, "I love you" before you drove away.

I could see the smile on your face maybe in your mind you felt there could be a chance for us to rekindle someday.

The Measure of Friendship

What is it to truly be someone's friend? Is it about being there when they need you even though your life seems at an end?

Is it smiling in their face when all you can do is talk about them behind their back? How can you live with yourself? Is there such a thing as honesty or is that something friends lack?

What is the measure of friendship? I really need to know! I struggle to find any purpose telling someone, "I appreciate you being in my life" when I rather say, "Just go."

Ahhhh... but I told them exactly how I felt! That is the measure of a friend. Being able to look at what honesty is really supposed to represent. See, to put a tag on friendship is to say that a friend isn't worth the time because I have to categorize what this is we share. Does it mean I'm always the one to break the ice but when I'm stuck you're never there?

The measure of friendship is really about how much love and respect we hold for someone. We have friends that we never talk to so how is that a friend? We have those we talk to everyday but when they're in need we quickly hideaway. Sometimes we hide so far underground it's impossible to see daylight again.

If I say, "You are my friend." It's because there will be a time when you need me and if I can't do anything more than let you know you're loved then that's what I will bend over backward to do. Not because I expect something in return but simply because my friendship with you is true.

The measure of friendship is most times not even determined with words. However, most times words suffice.

The measure of friendship is taking stock in someone besides our self being a valuable part of our existence, with a love that can never have a price.

To be a child again

Watching them at play I'm reminded what it was like for me; their tiny bodies of electricity running about; squeals of delight with all the energy and brightness of ten suns. At any given time ask them what game they are playing and surely will come the most elaborately detailed explanation of the simplest rendering for fun. Hide and Go Seek or Tag. It doesn't matter for whatever they play is done with stringent rules, yet in unison. They run awhile then sit. Funny how sitting about each other within earshot being totally engulfed in conversations that teeter on brilliance but has nothing to do with the game at hand or even world politics. Conversations so engrossing, they talk about school, bugs, plastic army men and Barbie dolls; or how the beat a level on a video game. They laugh, or fuss a little about important issues in their world. Without fear they hold innocence as a friendly hostage, knowing nothing about guilt and shame.

Then, as if shot out of a cannon, up and off they run! Seeking new adventures because there is a journey to be taken with everything they do. Children; so imaginative, tame yet wild and free!

Children; May you always remain young. May God bless the tender, rambunctious lives you'll lead?

A Letter to a Friend?

Tuesday, May 20, 2008

I don't know when it was that I began to see you in a much different light? I dare not tell you I had a dream of you last night. All I know is that today I feel you in my heart so deftly stronger than ever before.

And this scares me my friend because it leaves me wanting more.

They say the most meaningful relationships are built on foundations that hold through the test of time and began as friends. I never had the nerve to love that long or consider it could be done until you came into my life. Now what we are building is something only the Hands of God can create.

Something so fortified with love, trust and faithfulness it will be impossible for the strongest tribulations to shake.

When we accepted this relationship I don't think either of us really thought this would become a "thing".

I refused for awhile to look at you that way thinking separation is what an admission of love would bring.

But secretly I held you. So on nights when I needed to feel your touch even though we are miles apart from that kind of affection, I would read letters you have written to me and for that time your presence would comfort my heart through lyrical expression.

Well my friend where do we go from here now that I've admitted these things to you? Will I hide away like a frightened, bashful child or take ownership for my feelings that you so willingly allow me to feel?

I think I'll tell you just what I know in my heart is real...... one day.

Love, Your

Friend

Realizations

There is a fantasy world encountered in cyberspace where mere people are ensnared in this realm where everything is possible. I know because being one with such a vivid imagination it has become easy for me to see this as more than a fun medium of communication. I mean, look at this..... this thing of immense proportions that can put anyone of us with just the click of a button in touch with all walks of life in an instant. We can find lost friends or relatives. Maybe even find someone to love, with just a simple click and it is done. The only thing is most of these people live in foreign places or half way around the world. If you don't really have a social network of people that have domains then it's pretty much no chance finding anyone really......

Don't get me wrong. Cyberspace can be an exercise in futility; a learning place. It has allowed me this freedom to be creative and express that creativity in an open forum where once no one knew I breathed the same air or had this propensity to write; now my works can be viewed by masses of eyes. For that I am grateful. But let's look at cyberspace as a whole entity shall we?

There is from the planet of pop ups "getlaid2night.com", then from advertisement central "searchyouroldhighschoolfriends.org.", hell there is even for the desperate seekers from the planet of foreign affairs "justclickhere.uk." Yeah a million places to feed into the fantasies of endless relationships, sex and people we will probably never see or really get to know in this life.....EVER! I recently visited a site where it touted, "meet the person of your dreams!", "click" and God knows there I was trying to correspond with some woman that emailed me her phone number on the very first reply which went something like this: 009223466472-9! WHAT THE HELL IS THAT!? A SOCIAL SECURITY NUMBER!? Hell my phone don't even have that many numbers!

Not only that I emailed her back and low and behold she sends a response that she can't speak English! And here's the kicker! I honestly believed there could be a snowballs chance of surviving in hell that she and I would one day meet and miraculously fall in love! Oh my!! I know, I know... call me an idiot. Maybe I am, but I definitely am not the only one in cyberspace!

So what am I saying? Beats the hell out of me! I just know I have been rudely awakened from some kind of cryogenic sleep that when induced I lived comfortably in the seventies and Atari was still the video game pioneer with the coolest games and the only thing cyber was fiber optics! In that time I knew people and didn't have to imagine sex online through video chats or by visiting a pornography site. I could just look under my bed and retrieve a Playboy Magazine then have all the meaningless sex I chose! PHEW! Getting with the times is scary. Especially if cyberspace is what it's all coming down to...... "Click"

Feelings

Why do I feel this way about you?

Is it because you caress places inside my being that are much deeper than you touching my skin?

Or is it because you give me reason to believe in love when I thought my sensitivity to love was at an end?

Does it derive from the simplest pleasure I get from knowing what I mean to you?

Can it be that I've yearned for a woman to captivate me in everyway I allow you to?

Is it that just by hearing your voice I get heated with so much passion I can't help wanting your love?

Could it be that for once in my life I've been sent an angel to bless my soul with a power that can only come from heaven above?

I don't truly know the answers but I know it had to be you.

You are the only one that makes me feel this way by filling my heart with a love so true.

Kill Them All

While attending an AIDS rally one summer day, as the procession of marchers walked along the crowded street. "KILL THEM ALL!!!!" someone yelled from the crowd.

The voice sounded so angry. But why?

It wasn't enough that most of those who marched are stricken with this deadly disease.

Death looms over their lives in a constant battle that would tear most people apart and surely bring anyone to their knees.

The life of those infected as I saw it even though they live had from diagnosis reached an inappropriate end.

I mean, yes they functioned and breathed the same but no more children could they naturally have, selective partners would they be subjected to. And seclusion would claim many friends.

Why would someone say such a thing? Or hold such hatred in their heart?

Could it be that ignorance drives them to hate that which they do not understand? Or that fear tears their soul apart?

KILL THEM ALL!!" was yelled that day for everyone to hear and take heed to each word.

Why not "HEAL THEM ALL!" be shouted by every voice? That would be more emphatic, but to most believing this can happen is totally absurd.

Untitled III (True Friends)

Sometimes a girl will come and go.

But when a woman enters a man's life..... things begin to change.

He finds a friend that is more than any girl can ever be.

He realizes how important she is and respects her power to be free.

So he finds his own freedom.

Something that makes him want to give more of himself.

Some loosing in his being that allows him to put masculinity away on a far away shelf.

It has been said that "it takes a fool to learn that love don't love nobody."

But today I remember that love is supposed to be something wonderful.

To feel it grow inside ones heart and feel it's awesome dexterity and empowerment.

Love doesn't have to be a sexually intimate relationship.

It can be what makes good friends.

The Rest Of My Life

If I told you I was dying of a degenerative disease, what would be the reason you would want to be with me? Could you still be able to see, a strong, enduring man or would you see how truly lost I feel at times, and sympathize you will just to understand?

Or from a distance would you be near me? Will your feelings not be allowed to grow? Could you accept me for all that I'm worth and love me as if you didn't know?

Oh yes. I've felt the power of you loving me, even at those times we dare to say. I can see it in your eyes, feel it in your touch. The truth stands out even though words fade away.

If I told you I was afraid of running out of time and that it seems I may never get this chance to love again. That all my life so far you are the kind of love I prayed for; a woman who is my lover and my closest friend. What would you say? What would you do?

If I told you that I love you more than anyone I've loved before, and that I know I'd feel this way for the rest of my life. Would you honestly believe me or think I was bribing you to stay?

I love you with all my heart, all my essence right now. This is all I can do; with hopes that after I'm gone that love will still be felt by in your spirit as true, each and everyday.

Your Beauty I Still See

Open rays of light. Shine warm upon my skin.

Not the same rays that have shined every place in emptiness I've been.

Watching flowers bloom. To hear distant thunder boom.

Great mountains standing majestic.

Oceans depth beyond the rationale of this skeptic.

But where is the reasoning when too many answers swirl?

This creation seems so pale enclosed in this world.

Only in frustration dare I find.

The things in my mind that bring a smile to my lips.

Knowing all is not lost.

Fighting forth at all cost.

I know we are more than two passing ships.

So in that place where you are, I strive.... to be.

Living amidst the things of this world that are so very beautiful to me

When love has no boundaries

Space nor time exist......

Shadows belong and are seen through the fogs dense mist......

Is there wrong or right?

Can we win if there is no fight?

Do the emotions we store remain?

Well why do memories of lust overwhelm the brain?

There should be only tomorrows to live......

There is, and always should be, more of self to give......

And hate can not be found out of anger that sometimes arises......

Love keeps life standing solid on ever shifting ground.

What we don't see in ourselves (A letter from a 9 year old friend)

Dear Carlos,

You are an awesome person. You are right hopes & dreams do come true. Every time I look at your porch I smile & laugh. I have so many memories about you. Ever since you told me to emange (imagine) I have, hard! I am thinking about you and I know you are thinking about us. And if I were my mom I would date you. Your nice, funny, smart. And just remember you are an amazing person. And I know God will lead you to the right path.

Just try to keep this letter and this (a photograph of her)! I told you I would never leave but you left. It felt like I had someone in my life again.

Ps, keep this.

Love, Romana

Colors not Included

The first thing our eyes see in pictures is color. But I want you to visualize with your mind no colors so vibrant and true; no pastels of the rose blossoms petals, no lively green leaves and stems no irresistible blue hue of a silk ribbon.

Can you see this?

Is it as beautiful to you as it is to me?

I hope so because with you in my heart I don't need colors to know that color is there.

Your love for me is a prism that glows and fills my heart as only love is meant to do.

Colors not included? I beg to differ because the colors of my love for you always are.

Long Distance Love

A soft moment.....

When things are remembered and tenderly shared.

Like the first time you said," I love you", how proudly you said those words gave just a small example of how much you care.

So we take a toast together, even though we are miles apart......

I love you now just as before because you have grown like ivies and surrounded this once lonely heart.

Butterfly

How the world needs the gracefulness and royalty of butterflies; so eloquent, yet demanding; facing the world at large each day as if it were or could be the last. Being fruitful and determined, very understanding with a mission they multiply.

Only life is lived so fast.

Then the most extraordinary event occurs when through metamorphosis they change. From helpless caterpillar, to the force of nature butterflies can be their composition wonderfully re-arranged. And thus they fly forth doing what God intends.

Spreading glorious love along the way.

They are kings and queens these butterflies. We of this world need their beauty in every way, each and everyday. Stay strong, stay blessed, stay free!

One Last Cry

I close my eyes to keep the tears inside. The fears I can not hide. Separation has left my heart dry. You are out there living. I am here struggling on my own. Trying to keep faith that you still think of me and are faithful to what we had. Forcing jealousy to leave me alone and let me breathe.

Then you call just to say "hello" and hearing your voice for reasons I can't explain the tears swell in my eyes once more. Just knowing you're there has given me happiness again. You tell me to stay strong. You say you didn't mean to hurt me and you know I didn't mean to do the same to you. You offer a glimmer of hope by stating we may one day be together again. My hope. And like a boy with a first crush I blurt, "This time I'll try to be the man you want and need me to be! I love you!" Then, for an instant, silent hissing through the phones receiver.

Then just before the dial tone you say softly, "I will call you again sometime soon." and hang up. And once again I am missing you while disguising the tears in my eyes from sadness as those I may cry from pride.

Do you remember?

Do you remember the time we fought as if we were God born enemies? Or when my staying out all night long made you lock me out and the only way I got back in was to get on my knees and say, "please"?

Do you remember the passionate love we'd make? Pleasing each other with every inch of ourselves until our bodies ached? What about the nights we would just lay and talk for hours about silly things? Can you remember the joy us being together could bring into our hearts and lives?

Do you?

No matter what we have been through, no matter where we go either together or apart if you keep me in your heart you'll never forget.

Learning to Fly

Before I met you I was grounded.

All I did was pray for a blessing while I kept my head toward the sky.

Then God put you in my life.

Now everything feels so right. Everything is slowly coming together.

There is a peace and freedom you leave me feeling.

It's as if I am finally learning to fly.

82

How can I be sure?

What is this I feel? How do I know its love?

It is seeing you and losing all inhibition. It is having a conversation that is filled with everything I know because once I start talking to you I don't ever want to stop.

It's waking up each morning with you beside me and when you're not there wishing you were; wanting you more than I've ever wanted anyone or anything in my life.

Its this feeling I get inside that makes me smile even when I don't want to just from the mere thought of you. Or the queasiness that attacks my stomach as we talk about nothing or everything.

Those butterflies are there fluttering just like my heart.

It does get overbearing sometimes trying to comprehend this powerful emotion. But everything I feel in my heart and life about you is so very nourishing to my soul....... That's how I am sure.

An Ode to omo Ang'yele (my angel)

"I beheld the face of an angel on that fateful night. A face only an angel can have, ever so pleasing to my sight. Immediately, rational words eluded me, as if my mind had been taken away. The essence of her beauty relieved my troubled being and gave me escape to her world where there was nothing I really needed to say.

I briefly held her in my arms. And felt her soft, firm breast pressed to my chest. Her body heat subdued me; ensnaring me in her web of passion. I smelled her fragrance that captivated my senses; wanting her in my life while fearful that her answer would be an emphatic no. From that night to the next she held my heart as an oyster holds the most precious pearl.

We made love and the act so intense and deepening unleashed within me feelings I never imagined I'd have the chance to know. And even though we fell in love many fateful nights before, on this night we both knew the propensity for love was greater than she or I would ever be adult enough to show.

So here I sit this night alone now. I have spent days turned to dark loving her in memory; we are so many miles apart. The hurt I feel is not just for her love I lost but also because I allowed her to touch my heart.

And even though we will never see each other again as we did that fateful night, she will always be my angel."

A Rose in Bloom

You are a blooming rose.

With each day you become more unlimited to show the world how very beautiful you are. Also there is so much more to come.

You open up soft golden petals that had hidden the aura of womanhood you are here to exhibit.

Even still, what has so far been witnessed can only be recognized as wonderful.

Your dignity and integrity are gifts you should give to all that accept them. Your attitude and charisma are blessings for the lives of those that need a woman's strength to help us succeed.

Your life is a testimony.

God is alive in your heart. You fight on through life's struggles to be a good mother, friend and wife. You don't give up.

You are a blooming.

One day you'll have reached a level of maturity and self - confidence that will instill in you the meaning of exactly why you're her; and for what purpose.

One day you will understand what I and many others have always known, that you are so very beautiful inside your being as well as out. You will come to understand what having such true beauty as that you possess is really all about.

Snow

I don't believe anyone could know unless I told them just how badly I wish it would snow. To see the falling flakes of ice and feel winters chill. The icicles that form, hanging free. To sled carelessly down a hill as if being chased by time and swiftly eluding capture.

There is such a quieting effect when snow wraps around Gods earth. If one has not seen this then it would be impossible to know snows worth. Everything is peaceful and serene when snow blankets the ground. Like all the sound has been turned down and God is at rest.

Everything is so majestic. Life is calmed from the hectic daily grind. Then we all if we choose can relive our childhood playfulness building snow castles, or lying in the thickness of it and making angels. Having snowball fights that are fierce yet out of strictest enjoyment.

Then if you listen closely perchance you will hear, the lightest sound will pierce the air. The tree limb that cracks from the weight of ice. The tree that falls in the forest after it can no longer stand beneath the pressure. Sounds we can't ordinarily hear when the world is without snow.

In order to understand one must appreciate the wonder of falling snow and the beauty it brings, during that time all life stands still as God covers His creation with an angels soft, white wings.

Running

All my life I've been running.

Running from the law.

Running from people.

Running from this and that.

Not once did I realize all I was really doing is running out of time.

Neither did I realize God allowed me to run.

That what I've been through is by His grace and mercy and would eventually be for His glory.

God knew even though I didn't have a clue that one day I would want Him to change my life.

But once I got tired He took those running shoes off my feet.

He settled me down.

It took some time but He knew I would one day come around.

See, God held out his hand to me at the lowest point I'd ever been in my life.

He told me "He loved me no matter what I've done".

He accepted me with all my faults and fears and still He sought to bless me as soon as I let Him in.

God has given me a peace in my life.

Something I never thought I could have.

Greater than anything I could ever afford.

So here I stand a testament of His mercy, love and grace. I don't regret all the running I did. But I sure was tired!

However it turned out in my life it was worth it because it is for Gods purpose.

I know it is not about who runs the fastest it's about the ones that endure who ultimately win.

Through the life I lived before I was taught to be a soldier, to fight hard for everything I achieve.

It has prepared me for my salvation and for spending the rest of my life in eternity.

If You Love Someone

There is a saying, "if you love someone set them free and if they return then surely it is meant to be".

I've walked out of many women's lives, never to return and most times neither did they return to me.

I just stopped coming around or doing little things.

I've said what I did was right. I've found all the faults, dealt with my insecurity.

I've smiled and lied, never actually saying goodbye for fear of finality.

I've played the games not hoping to score, wore blinders so I couldn't see.

But here I am telling you I must set you free while hoping that it's understood

I hope you return to me. Though in my soul I know it will not happen that way.

Reality is when you love someone you don't give them away, you cherish them.

You build, you admire, and you fight hard to have meaning and purpose with them.

I could just walk away from you tonight or you walk away from me.

But what will that prove? And to set you free is easier?!

Then set by waiting patiently like a fool?

Instead I ask do you want me in your life and why? Then together we

can figure out what to do, if there is a remedy. If not, face to face this time

I'll be man enough to say "goodbye".

Without heartache or a losers misery.

Axis

"I cried before, as a child.
Receiving injuries that children are prone to or because I
misbehaved and wore my daddy's beating. I cried as a child hating
green vegetables yet my mom made me eat them. And sometimes
when I was sick I cried because I was afraid. I grew up with so
many mixed emotions, in many different family environments,
with many different members. I attended funerals and there I cried
even though I didn't fully understand why. The funny thing is....
when I became a man (so to speak) at the ripe age of 13 I stopped
crying. And this caused pain, fear and confusion to take on a
different meaning inside my being. I withstood the injuries
associated with being adventurous at play. But I was unprepared to
deal with loneliness, broken hearts and growing pains that kept me
crying inside my heart. Now as an adult male, funny that I having
undergone a conversion of sorts cry now just because I can feel.
Watching a sad movie, I cry. Talking to my lover about how much
she means to me, I cry. I Feel lonely sometimes and I cry.... only
with each tear I cry outwardly the better I feel inside my soul."

"I Love You"

When I say "I love you".........

Do you feel it? I mean truly feel that you know what I say is for real?

Does it make your heart race and chills run down your spine?

Can you understand because of love everything we do together will work out just fine?

Are my words endless according to the love you need me to give?

Does it confirm why you've chosen to spend the rest of this life with only me?

Or is it deeper than the ocean, farther than the eyes can see?

Maybe it means nothing to you at all?

I just take for granted that me telling you this makes it all OK?

When I say "I love you" its not because I have to...... but because you give me reason to love you and your love for me is what allows me to feel this way.

If Ever The Sunrises

There is a certain Beauty in sunrises. To find that special place where ones vision of this magnificent event is unimpeded. Then to witness the dawning of a new day...... amazing!

"If ever the sunrises and your love is not in my life.

My days shall forever come filled with hurt.

There would be no joy, no laughter, nothing but an emptiness beyond anything I could ever feel.

If ever the sunrises and your love is not in my life.

Oh baby..... my life would forever be lived in vain.

I would only have fond memories of what true love is.

Its power and majesty with you being in my life.

And because I could never forget, those memories would drive me insane."

Together in the Heart

(This was written for a fellow inmate during my incarceration in a Florida Correctional Institution. 1997)

One glass and a chilled bottle of wine sit on the table and you drink alone.

Staring at a rose you bought yourself. Wishing I was home.

Wondering how much longer will you have to be by yourself?

Hating me as the minutes pass "bye" another period of time you have to put   your love on the shelf.

I know me being here leaves you with life to undergo without me.

Raising the kids, paying the bills. I know you cry at night wishing I were free.

But baby, please hold on. And know I am there with you.

I'd never be too far away.

Because I am in your heart and soul as long as you love me.

There is where I'll stay.

Carrying the weight (A poem to all that endure incarceration from the outside)

You carry the weight of our world on your shoulders and I thank you with all the love I can give right now.

If it weren't for you I'd have nothing but time and empty space. Because of you I have everything I need.

Helping Me

Your love helps me through this journey.

You give me strength to succeed.

You fill my heart through the lonely days.

You tend to my every need.

You put up with my sorrow.

You help me to get over my grief.

You are more than a woman to me.

You reassure my belief.

You are my lover.

You are my woman.

You are my best friend.

You are my lady and I pray you never change.

With you by my side what I can accomplish has no foreseen end.

106

Bound

We are bound by an emotion greater than

anything in this world. A simple four

letter word that says we care for

each other.

Deeper than the ocean.

More beautiful than a strand of pearls.

This tie that binds us together is stronger

Than any that would try and tear us apart.

Its the love we hold for each other

That has us bound together

yet sets us free in our hearts.

Ever Think......

Ever think about how things happen in your life? Situations that come about? People you meet? To wake up from the sleep of death in the morning. How did it actually happen?

So many of us take these tremendous blessings for granted. Like finally getting that long awaited raise from a thankless job. Or having children that are born with ten fingers and toes. Complete. The clothes we wear and the food we eat.

The smiles that greet us from passing faces of people we don't know. The mumbled curses. The cars we drive. The accidents that occur. Each and every single thing upon this planet that grows. How does it hap - pen?

Wow! what is there not to be thankful for?

Well maybe someone has a broken heart because a lover has gone away? Or a broken life that just seems to not get fixed? Maybe a loved one has passed on leaving behind unwanted debt and dismay?

Or maybe someone has been diagnosed to have a life threatening condition? So many questions, so many scenarios of things that should bring us to our knees. I read a sign one day that said, "If you don't know where you are going..... you might not get there".

Today is really all we have. Right now is all the time afforded. And we live. We strive. We reach out for something substantial. Going places most will never dare.

We should be appreciative of this chance at life we are given no matter what each day may bring. It's okay to wonder what does this all mean. Just don't stand and wait for an answer because then we miss out on everything.

Seasons Change

I long 4 the warmth of days gone "bye". When there was a sparkle in my eyes and everything I wanted 2 achieve was within my reach. Now all that remain are those memories in time........ My life is so empty without a woman 2 love by my side. Someone I can give my heart 2. Someone 2 help me strive......... Whenever I get the nerve 2 go out and meet someone new. It doesn't work and eventually falls apart because they don't want the same things from life and love that I do........ So loneliness keeps me attached 2 the proverbial ball and chain. Crying in my heart 4 freedom, 4 love. As the seasons change.

I can remember all 2 well the nights I'd close my eyes, praying 4 a woman so strong that would be in my life 4 all time. But then I am forced 2 think of the love I have given 2 so few. And water fills my eyes because I have hurt so many........ So how can I expect 4 me love will be so true. I still keep hope that love will one day come my way again, bring back that sparkle 2 my life. Hopefully next time it will come 2 stay........ But until then I'll live with loneliness as we watch the seasons change.

The way I lived and treated love in my past has cursed my heart. When now all I want is 2 be able 2 love. Is that so wrong? Am I emotionally 2 far detached?....... I do know that the seasons keep coming and going. While love in my life has gone.

Something

There is something about you I often find myself wishing I was given the chance to know.

Something about you I believe is as warm as a summer's breeze and softer than fresh fallen snow.

I'm grateful to see you when I do. Your smile ignites my heart, reaching deep into my soul.

So this is to bless you with joy, peace and prosperity in the coming years.

May God be with you and your family in everything you do and wherever life leads you to go.

Troubled

My soul is in trouble Lord! So I come to you to set me straight!
My old self keeps telling me "I ain't ready!", but how can I not be
ready?! I have been prepared for this day since birth. I've been
living in the world for far too long. I keep allowing myself to live
accustom to this world when I know better. I know for me life
would be much more meaningful if I lived according to your word.
But I still stumble and fall. I sin! When I know that sin will take
me to hell! I hurt inside Lord because I know I am not worthy of
the love and mercy You bestow upon me time and time again. I'm
afraid because the strong man I think myself to be is often weak
and fragile to temptations and so I go astray. I am foolish because I
refuse to recognize something as simple as belief. And I don't have
faith in You.

I can't lie to myself anymore and say that "I love the Lord with
all my heart" because truth is I cherish the things of the world. I am
afraid to give them up because the lie dwelling inside me says "I'll
have nothing if I do". It's a lie and I know it! So I ask You Lord to
help me believe in You. I need to feel You in my life! I have
known sin personally now I desire to know You in the very same
way. You already know more about me than I could ever know
about myself, this is why I am asking you to manifest in me the
person I truly am. The man You made me to be. I want to be right!
I want to be made a new creation in this old, used body! I don't
have any other options on my own. I am asking You Lord to loose
me from this world that binds me. Help me to walk in Your spirit.
You are stronger and more capable to lead me. Without You
holding my hand and guiding me..... I am lost.

Expecting to Live

We only think about living. From the time we are capable to have rational thoughts we begin to take for granted that life will come each day. The mere prospect of death, no one desires to even contemplate that as we live surely we shall die.

My God! The healthy beings are so fortunate! They are afforded to roustabout as if there is no such thing as a carnal demise. They wake up each morning and carry out daily task having no concern that one day, at anytime.... they will live no more. They act as if life is a guaranteed occurrence with no end.

But for those of us born with or that have acquired life threatening illnesses the prospect of dying becomes more evident. Yes, we live as if there is no consideration of death. We rise just as everyone else on a daily basis. We go about our days wearing a mask of confidence and strength. But we have within our sub - conscience that impending thought that today could be our last. We learn to disguise the fear.

We come to appreciate every second of life far from the mundane expectancy to live. We find gratitude. Even still, just as everyone we have no idea when or how the end will come. So we plod as if mortality is in our corner, cheering us on, sheltering us from an inevitable fate. Just like everyone else. We all live, no matter circumstance, we live with little regard for the day we will surely die.

Summer

She looks at me.

And like the sun rises in the eastern sky, my world begins to shine.

Her gaze warms my heart.

Her smile blinds my apprehension.

Her touch allows me to believe love is mine.

When we kiss.

A heat flares out of coldness.

When we touch, my skin perspires.

Likes reeds of grass moistened by dew.

She intensely adorns me with her yearning

I gladly accept her passion.

This woman of love.

She fills my being.

Breezes of joy that caress my soul, gently blowing away my fear.

She is quick to always be a woman.

With a stifling humidity she upholds this.

Even in the late hours when no one is around she is still a lady.

So charming and elegant.

So royal.

So serene.

Like the coming of a starry summer night.

She lay down all inhibitions.

To please me she goes to any length.

Nothing does she hold back it is her only yen to fulfill my every erotic dream.

And underneath the moonlit sky we still our throbbing bodies to rest.

Her head softly upon my chest.

A whisper of love in my ear......

A Thousand Miles Away

Nobody ever said loving someone would be easy.

I looked for love in many faces. Thought love would come from mere physical acts.

They have told me "love is everywhere and in everything".

But why is it so hard for me to see?

They say that "love is stronger than anything known to man".

But why for love do I get so weak?

I met her and immediately wanted her in my life even though we had never seen each other except for pictures on a computer screen.

I told myself this was different.

I told myself love has no boundaries or limitations except those I place upon it.

And again I believed...... in love.

I realize today that love can not be seen with carnal eyes.

Real love can only be seen with the eyes of ones heart.

That gives substance and helps to have faith in that which to the flesh can not be felt when the one we love is a thousand miles away.

Kimberly

This may very well be the hardest piece I will ever write......

When we met I was just a wandering soul.

Trying to find my way in a world that had for me changed so much from what I knew it to be.

She was an accomplished mature woman that I never saw being with such a man as me.

A man of intemperate disposition. So angry, stubborn and caught up in the past of my life.

But she took my heart into loving hands and gave me something I felt unworthy to receive.

Without having touched my skin or seen the pain in my eyes when I cry. She soon agreed to be my wife.

I would fight her loving me, so furiously. Not physically. But by not accepting her love as real.

I saw the hurt in her eyes when I acted like her love was nothing to me. Yet, she continued to teach me how to feel.

Unconditional takes on a new meaning when it comes to how deeply her love for me went.

She held me in her arms knowing I am ill. She safeguarded my heart with her own even when I tried to hurt myself. I know now her love is heaven sent.

Only an angel could tolerate a foolish man.

Only an angel could stay.

She wiped away tears from my contorted face and reassured me that her love would never go away.

Through the hard times she held onto me.

And I held onto her. We held onto love and the hope it would set us both free.

In the end it has proven that nothing can separate us as friends.

For her I am eternally grateful. For her love I would do it all again..... but change one thing......

Love her more.

Because then I would know how to love her like she is meant to be cherished.

Or for the next woman to come into my life I have this lesson learned.

Don't ever take love and a woman's power to love for granted. It is something most certainly any man must earn.

Standing up again

I have been knocked down. But not until I choose to stay there am I ever truly down for good. I stand!

In the face of adversity. I stand!

I cry sometimes from life's pain. Losing and gaining. Fighting and giving up. Hurting so bad that nothing seems to ease the misery.

But a smile. Maybe a hug. Maybe nothing tangible but to know I live.

I STAND!

OOPS! I just got knocked back down! Give me a second to catch my breath......

Phew! I stand!

I............ STAND!!!! Closer to God when I stand! Closer to my dreams.......

I STAND!

126

Positivity

August 8, 2000

Dear diary,

I found out today that I am dying. I didn't know how to react. Funny thing is I didn't freak out! When the doctor told me the news I felt as though I expected it. My heart raced momentarily and palms got clammy. I could feel sweat trickling from my armpits. But it only lasted a couple minutes then everything was alright. I sat there on the examination table with my hands cuffed between my knees. I don't know..... Was I suppose to do something or act a certain way? The doctor asked "how do you feel?", and I said "fine." She asked if I wanted to talk to a psychologist. Explaining that most people given life and death news like this usually need to talk to a professional about how they feel. I just looked at her with a smile and said," No. I'll be fine." The sad thing is she cried. She came over hugged me so tightly and cried. I put an arm around her and told her it will be alright. She said it makes her think about her own mortality. She said if she hadn't been my doctor for all those years it would be different possibly easier for her to handle. I could only say, "It will be alright.". I said a prayer. I can't remember what it was exactly, just prayed.

Everyday It Rains

Even when the sun is shining still in my heart it rains.

I don't know if this will make sense to you but I live with constant pains.

On the outside I wear a crooked smile. I hold my chest out and my head up.

I greet those I encounter with open arms. I am such a hypocrite!

At night when all the worlds asleep I toss and turn from grief.

Storms rage inside my mind that offer no relief.

Those that know me are fast to say I am a very passionate man. Honest and respectful. Witty and intelligent. Cool.

But they only see the face that I adorn on the outside. Not the one inside that makes me feel like a fool.

I don't tell anyone that I am bombarded with torrential rain. I dare not let anyone too close.

Not even the ones that love me most.

Everyday it rains.

Even when the sun shines bright. It still continues to rain inside my soul.

I once was a promising young man, now I am feeble and old.

Who am I to be so gifted? Who am I to be so proud?

Where are the words that say I am grateful, I think them yes, but am cautious to say them aloud.

Here I sit trying to find something meaningful in everything.

Even in the rain.

Looking for answers. Hoping for freedom.

Desiring a most humble and lasting change.

For me everyday it rains. Even when the sun is shining.

That's just how it is to be.

I am however, so grateful.

Grateful that life has been given to someone as unimportant as me.

Wanting

Like a chill of air rushing over me.

Unable to smile wiping my nose, crying inside hard lonely tears.

Longing for closeness in body. I have so much in my mind.

Edgy, unpredictable, sensuous.

Looking into the eyes that pass for recognition. Hoping.

If only for a moment in time just to be held within the perimeters of someone else's dreams.

Amorous.

Where is my cupid floating lost in the vastness of space and time?

Passionately complaining that there is nothing left.

Spiritually feeling everything my heart desires.

Cursing how damned cold it is.

No more logs to keep a fire.

Who said it is better to have ones self as a friend?

It gets tiresome and unfeeling after awhile.

Sensitivity turns to burning pain of flesh rubbing viciously upon flesh.

Falling snow. Light freezing rain mixed in.

Comfy cozy in my home sheltered from the....... need.

Yet, in my home there is me..... alone.

Speckled meanderings of an aging man.

Unsatisfied attempts to discard selfish greed.

Maybe it's not winter after all?

Maybe it is deathly heated summertime fury?

Maybe I have been knocked unconscious from the hardness of the fall?

And now I dream of..... a woman.

The one I saw looking at me while I ate a hamburger at Burger King.

How I hate Burger King.

But she was so very sexy. Nothing beautiful about her could I see pass her bodily frame.

Damn.

Wanting to feel the coming warmth of spring.

Knight in shining armor

I am a knight in shining armor.

There is my damsel in distress a million miles away.

Still, I begin my journey.

Swimming across the width of many seas.

Climbing mountainous heights never before imagined by mortal men.

And there come upon the fire breathing dragon.

Vicious. Angry dragon.

Slaying it. I cut off its gnarled, calloused head as a trophy.

I will display before my damsel as a testament of this arduous task.

Hoping it will show my fortitude.

Still more to complete.

I scale the castle wall that protects her from freedom.

Breaking through the sturdiness of a barricaded dungeon cell door.

She awaits my rescue.

Our eyes meet.

She is exactly what I hoped her to be.

Now I must prove to her beyond that which has been done that I am

the man deserving enough to receive her most cherished possession......

...... her love.

And now my journey takes on another form.

For the deed is not yet done.

Worthiness, faithfulness and devotion lie ahead that I must adhere to.

If she is to be my queen and I her king.

Love Is.....

Love is in everything and everywhere. It has no limitations or
boundaries except those we as humans place upon it. So we can
not see its worth and longevity merely with carnal eyes. It can only
be truly seen with the eyes of ones heart.

Between Us

If I could make things right

I would take your shattered heart and heal it with my love

I would expose myself to you and hope...... hope, that you'll see the man I yearn to be.

Not the person I was

I would cry for you

tear down the walls that hide me from you

If I could only make things right

then for your love there is nothing I would not do.

I would not fear that you will want more than I can give

Me allowing you into my life and heart,

the happiness you bring

all that I can not say will be proof enough for you to know,

it is for your love I live.

If I could make things right,

there would be no sadness when we say
"goodbye"

because without a doubt I know

you would be returning to me,

moving as fast as you can to get back to me

138

just like each day the sun without fail,

returns to the lonely sky.

I would love you more than any man can or ever will again

If I could only make things right

and all else fails,

I would know how to accept that all we will ever be is friends.

Far from......

I'm far from being this wonderful man many say I am

I'm just a simple man..... nothing special about my life at all

I talk about how I feel today

I laugh when I fall.

I cry in the dark loneliness of my heart

I sing songs of love in the shower or while I attend to my affairs.

I imagine her eyes looking into my soul

her fingers smoothing softly over my hair.

I see the worth in many people yet, I can't see my own

I encourage when I feel weak,

I uplift if not but only one heart

even when I don't want to, hiding from hurt in the safety of my home.

I am far from being this wonderful man so many say that I am......

I could say I need You

I could say I need you.

But what will this prove to anyone but me?

What then?

Will you be sympathetic to my loneliness?

Could you truly feel as I do and agree?

Is there really togetherness when we are so many miles apart?

Am I being foolish baby?

Please answer the question.....

Maybe then I will understand.

All I want is the emptiness to leave my heart.

But not at someone else's expense.

If I say I need you am I being real with me?

How can I need you?

You belong to someone else.......

Damn.

When I physically want to feel you, I can't.

I can't make love to you passionately.

It will only cause more turmoil in your life,

If I say "I need you",

But I do.

However I must accept it will not be right.

It would be okay if all you had was baggage.

But even though I would...... I could never honestly love another mans wife.

How do I trust that in the end,

you will remain faithful to me?

Why am I even thinking this?

I can say I need you, but after that where will you and I be?

Happiness

She told me, "I just want to make you happy."

It didn't sound far fetched at the time.

In fact I felt honored that she would want to give me joy,

instead of play tricks with my mind.

But I know now she could only do so much.

I also know nothing works if we don't try.

Happiness is something we feel inside our beings.

It is the smiles we get that make us warm up ,

The hugs we get when we cry.

I remember as a child, one Christmas getting that red fire truck with the extendable ladder!

Wow! That was me being happy.

Can't remember a damn thing about the emotion after that,

It hurts too much trying to grow to something I can not feel.
Wanting to know if being truly happy exist is more than I can see.

I have been told I have so much to be happy for.

Or that a man like me should know exactly what happiness is about.

But I ask, "how can you be so sure that I have this knowledge when in my heart happiness has caused such doubt?"

So I seek to find happiness,

if not then how will anyone be allowed to share this wonderful feeling with me?

I lost it somewhere along the way

God knows I want to find it again

that is the only way my heart, my mind and soul,

will be able to live free.

So this angel that God gave to me I let walk right out of my life.

I did not cry.

Not then. Didn't shed a single tear.

I know she wanted only the best for me,

and this was happiness. The one thing besides love I fear.

Broken Image

I look at myself in the mirror.

Is my hair neat enough?

Wow..... look at my face!

I'm much older. More chiseled. Harder.

Straggled images in my eyes. These blank eyes.

Wanting to see where the time went.

I stare at the reflection.

Once so full of promise.

So handsome.

There was life in these eyes.

This body owned life!

Long before everything else existed.

Warm red blood coursed through my veins.

From chapped, uneven lips that hid discouraging teeth..... I smiled.

Now. Everything I see tells unbelievable lies.

I gaze hard and long trying to see through the mask that conceals the real me.

Why can't I find............................. me?

Why has the blinders of time hidden the man I long to recognize?

Maybe the reason is that I truly don't know who I am.

I have been so many things in my lifetime.

Looking into the mirror I know that everything I've been has nothing to do with who I am supposed to be.

So I finally walk away because I find it uncomfortable to look at the person I have become.

I Am.....

A warm rain on a hot summer's day

A slow moving storm with lightening flashes illuminating dark clouds,

far away

A tattered warrior coming home from battle bruised, tired, proud and hard

A yielding kiss to a lovers lips

just before the passion of lust takes hold and emotions become painful

scars

A flightless bird scurrying about the ground

A mute person trying desperately to speak aloud

A circus with many performers, yet there is no clown

I am a divergence at the end of a winding road

A gust of wind propelling a large boats sail

there is no direction as it simply floats

A angry beast bearing down for the kill

A starry night when everything is still

Love.

Hate.

Peace.

Tears.

Joy.

A child that has broken a favorite toy

I am a man who is many things like a chameleon I adapt with a
subtle change

A man of endurance and strength

A vast mountain range.

I'd still be on my knees

So many nights I spent on my knees praying for you.

"Please God send her to me. I need to feel her love.

Or my emotions will be bound throughout eternity. I

know I am so unworthy, a child trapped in the body of a man

but for her I will grow to be all the man she needs."

For far too many years I was held captive by loneliness.

A prisoner with no hope, no dreams, no purpose.

My heart aching so badly. My tears drowning me in sorrow.

I prayed for you to come and rescue me.

Help me to love. To see better tomorrows.

Then one day you appeared out of thin air. Like a wind that blows.

No one knows which direction it comes from or what direction

it goes. You simply appeared.

At first my immaturity was my undoing, yet you kept giving me your

heart.

You would get frustrated by my insecurity and distrust.

But you refused to let that tear us apart.

And like an ivy we grew..... together.

We endured the bad times, found more love through the good.

We became the kind of friends that last.

 Because when it comes to what we have, we always do what
we should.

In that my being has been elevated to heights I never knew exist.

I learned to have faith in someone else.

How not to be judgmental or hard on myself.

I have learned many lessons on what unconditional love entails.

My prayers have been answered.

 I can hold my head up high, just from the strength you give to me.

 I am no longer afraid because my heart has been opened to love
and the loneliness I felt has been given reprieve.

I love you....... as if my life depends on this love to survive.

I was a sinking man in a sea of hardness.

God threw me the lifeline........ You.

Now it is for your love and happiness I strive.

Open Heart Surgery; Healing

Sometimes I cry. There hasn't to be a reason why. The tears just begin to fall.

Sometimes I want love so bad, even when I already have it. It's just that days come which I want it more than someone is able to give.

I have tried but can't find happiness because I have been blinded to what happiness truly means. I smile, laugh. Tell jokes. But inside my being too many broken hearts have built a wall of protection that will not allow anything such as joy, to come in.

The comatose state of my being has for years been what keeps me oblivious to the pain...... of loss.

There are mindful impulses of course.

A broken heart can not just be ignored. Like I am totally numb.

No. It does hurt. So bad that I just want nothing to do with hurting like that ever again. But what kind of wish is it for one to have that they never experience love? Does it really ache so deeply that I can honestly admit such emotion has no place in my life and heart? And why would I cheat myself of journeying through all that life and love have to offer?

Seeing that I am human. I understand some things I have to go through in order to make me better. Stronger. These hurts and disappointments had to come because they are lessons. Learning how to love or, how not to. Being taught what is right and what is wrong. To trust and be faithful. To care.

With life there are only two guarantees. We will live from the time we are conceived in the womb. And surely we will die. Everything in between is merely chances taken to make sense out of the life we have been afforded.

Open heart surgery..... wow. This actually means I have to open my heart to accept love. It means I have to take chances with others. Trying to find pleasure and contentment within someone else's heart. Its never easy venturing into the unknown but if having experiences before then surely there should be familiarities the next time around. Thus I should show some form of growth. Either it is becoming more stoic toward certain things or more stern as to my beliefs about those things taking form in my life.

We have all witnessed the relationships that endure. Those that we deem will never end but are proved wrong by surprise when it does. We have all taken part of relationships we thought were meant to be. Those that we felt so strongly would be the only relationship ever to come our way. And we have clung to those that have hurt immeasurably. We have cried so many tears after countless operations that left abysmal scars upon our hearts. We have found elation from people we never imagined could harm us much less do in the end.

But.... we somehow continue receiving numerous surgeries; each one more prolific than the last. We shut down and then like a raging wind another surgeon comes and we permit our hearts to undergo their treatments. Most times without warning we open our lives. We plead the old wounds to heal. For there is within us that glimmer of hope, that this time will be the last. But one never knows nor will ever know unless we are willing to let go of preconceived notions about love.

About The Author

Most of Open Heart Surgery was composed while serving time in a Florida prison 1996-2000. I had always imagined what the love of a woman was about. Love used to be a tool I used to get what I wanted from women which usually involved sex. However during my incarceration and events after my release I began to see this powerful emotion in a different light. My writings then became plea's for the kind of love I one time ran from or was afraid to be involved with. Open Heart Surgery is conversations, letters, thoughts, and feelings about my life of love and writing. It is the essence of my heart as I display it daily to the world and those closest in my life. It is my way of understanding and finding answers to all the questions tossed around in my head about the greatest of emotions.

"Therefore abides hope, faith and love. These three, but the greatest of these is love." I Corinthians 13:13 (Harper New American Standard Study Bible)

Coming Soon....

By Carlos Robinson

Excerpt from Ghetto Blessings

I Am so Blessed

........To have lived so long a sinner. To have fallen on my knees
and prayed for God to touch my heart and forgive me. Many times.
To ask Him to love me and accept my soul enough to save.

Having people in my life that love me regardless of my past. Loving me so much they can't just turn away. People that stand beside me, adore me and encourage me to live for brighter days.

........To know emotions so strong, when I felt such emotions were a lie. To realize my pain, understand the reason for the tears I cried inside.

........To finally smile for joy, even weep for happiness I one time couldn't receive. To have the shackles of sin removed from my being and from all the misery God allowed me to be relieved.

........Lord knows I give my best most times to keep Him in my sight. To hold His hand and be close to Him, keeping faith that everything no matter how bad it seems will one day be alright.

........I still fall sometimes but not as hard as I used to. I still sin sometimes but I can pray today for forgiveness when I do.

........To have God in my life keeping me strong. Guiding me. Giving me hope in each day that comes when to me those days seem so few.

........Now I live with purpose. In my heart there are better things to feel. I am so blessed by Gods grace, mercy and love. It's good to finally believe that such holy things are real.

........Though I may not always show it, each day I open my eyes I give God my praise. I am blessed to stand up in the face of fate and be a man so brave.

........Having God keep moving in my life in a glorious and mighty way. I am so blessed! To be a soldier on the battlefield keeping Satan from being victorious each day.

........I am so blessed to love, have joy, fight through pain, and prevail over times so rough when I could not see any good. To have persevered and to fight hard each moment with everything I've got within me to make my salvation in someone's heart easily understood.

www.ingramcontent.com/pod-product-compliance
Lightning Source LLC
Chambersburg PA
CBHW021113090426
42738CB00006B/621